TOP 25

SOCCER SKILLS, TIPS, AND TRICKS

JEFF SAVAGE

Enslow Publishers, Inc.
40 Industrial Road
Box 398
Berkeley Heights, NJ 07922
USA

http://www.enslow.com

Library of Congress Cataloging-in-Publication Data

Savage, Jeff, 1961–
  Top 25 soccer skills, tips, and tricks / Jeff Savage.
      p. cm. — (Top 25 sports skills, tips, and tricks)
  Includes index.
  Summary: "Explores soccer skills, including the basic techniques for passing, shooting, dribbling, and defense,
and provides tips, drills, and fun tricks for young people to practice their game"—Provided by publisher.
  ISBN 978-0-7660-3860-8
  1. Soccer—Handbooks, manuals, etc.—Juvenile literature. I. Title.
  GV943.S25 2012
  796.334—dc22

                          2010040351

Paperback ISBN 978-1-59845-359-1

Printed in the United States of America

052011 Lake Book Manufacturing, Inc., Melrose Park, IL

10 9 8 7 6 5 4 3 2 1

Do not attempt the more advanced skills and tricks without adult supervision.

To Our Readers:
We have done our best to make sure all Internet addresses in this book were active and appropriate when we went to press.
However, the author and the publisher have no control over and assume no liability for the material available on those Internet
sites or on other Web sites they may link to. Any comments or suggestions can be sent by e-mail to comments@enslow.com or
to the address on the back cover.

♻ Enslow Publishers, Inc., is committed to printing our books on recycled paper. The paper in every book contains 10% to
30% post-consumer waste (PCW). The cover board on the outside of each book contains 100% PCW. Our goal is to do our part
to help young people and the environment too!

Illustration Credits: AP Images / Alberto Pellaschiar, p. 30; AP Images / David Ramos, p. 26; AP Images / Hassene Dridi,
p. 7; AP Images / Jonne Roriz, p. 43; AP Images / Mark Baker, p. 29; AP Images / Rebecca Blackwell, p. 25; AP Images / Sara
D. Davis, p. 17; © Asia Images Group Pte Ltd / Alamy, p. 11; Cathy Cesario Tardosky, pp. 5, 9 (bottom), 12, 15, 37; Enslow
Publishers, Inc., p. 4 (field diagram); © Kirk Strickland / iStockphoto.com, p. 1; Shutterstock.com, pp. 4, 9 (top), 10, 13, 18,
19, 21, 23, 27, 31, 33, 35, 36, 39, 41, 44; © Ulrich Doering / Alamy, p. 42.

Cover Illustration: © Kirk Strickland / iStockphoto.com (Young soccer player kicking the ball).

CONTENTS

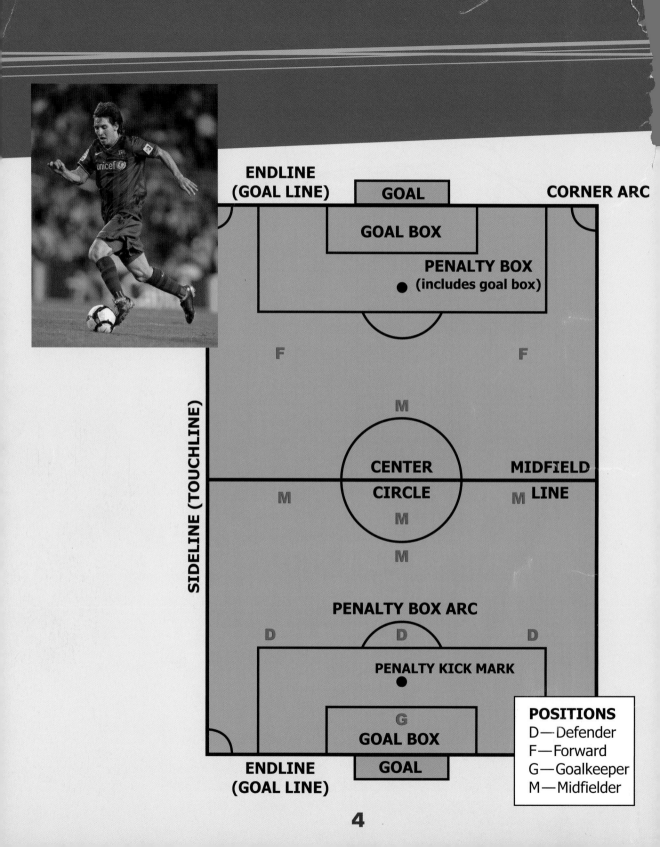

ENDLINE
(GOAL LINE)

GOAL

CORNER ARC

GOAL BOX

PENALTY BOX
(includes goal box)

F

F

SIDELINE (TOUCHLINE)

M

CENTER
CIRCLE

MIDFIELD
LINE

M

M

M

M

PENALTY BOX ARC

D

D

D

PENALTY KICK MARK

G

GOAL BOX

ENDLINE
(GOAL LINE)

GOAL

POSITIONS
D—Defender
F—Forward
G—Goalkeeper
M—Midfielder

CONTROLLING THE BALL

The object in soccer is to score more goals than your opponent. You can score only if you have the ball. There are several ways that you can gain and keep control of the ball.

1 DRIBBLING

Basic dribbling is a critical soccer skill. You must learn how to move the ball forward across open space with your feet. To do so, you should tap the ball with the inside or outside edge of your foot. You cannot control the ball as well with your toes. Learn to dribble equally with either foot. Keep the ball close to your feet. Do not kick the ball and run to it. Take no more than two steps between taps. When dribbling, it is important to see your opponents and teammates. Learn to dribble without watching the ball. Keep your head up. You can practice dribbling on your own. Run forward as fast as possible while keeping control of the ball.

It is important to use both feet when dribbling and to keep your head up so you can spot an open teammate.

2 CHANGING DIRECTION

You will not always have open space to dribble. An opponent might suddenly be blocking your path. You must change directions to move past your opponent. To decide whether to go left or right, watch your opponent. If he or she is standing slightly one way, go the other. Go in the same direction as his or her forward foot. If your opponent is standing squarely at you, it is time to use a trick move. Here are four trick moves you can choose from:

- **Inside turn**—You can make an inside turn by stepping over and just past the ball, pushing it with your instep and moving in another direction.
- **Outside turn**—You can make an outside turn by pushing the ball with the outer edge of your foot and moving in that direction.
- **Scoop move**—You can use the scoop move by using the outer edge and last few toes of your foot to lift the ball up and over your opponent's feet.
- **Step-over move**—You can use the step-over move (also called the "scissors") by swinging your foot just above the ball in a passing or shooting motion, then pushing the ball away with the outside of either foot in the other direction.

When an opponent is blocking your path, change directions to move past the defender. You can make an outside turn with the outside of your foot like this player (white jersey).

3 CHANGING SPEED

Shifting directions does not always work. Opponents figure out your speed and adjust their defense. This is when switching pace can fool your opponent. You can slow down to maintain possession for another moment while your teammate gets open for a pass. Or you can slow down in order to lull your opponent into thinking you are about to pass, then speed up again. In this case, you want to be obvious when you slow down. Crouch your body and lean forward. Wait for your opponent to close in. Then take off in a burst of speed.

In a real trick move called the stop-and-start, you can switch speeds and fake a change of direction at the same time. Dribble fast in one direction. Then stop the ball with the bottom of your foot and turn your body in another direction. As your defender shifts to block your new direction, explode in your original direction.

PRO TIPS AND TRICKS

Cristiano Ronaldo of Portugal was the 2008 Federation Internationale de Football Association (FIFA) World Player of the Year. Ronaldo is nicknamed "King of the Step-over." Ronaldo performs the step-over like a smooth dance move. With his left foot, he hovers over the ball in a circular motion and plants it on the left side of the ball. With the outside edge of his right foot, he cuts the ball to the right and past his opponent.

When you change directions while dribbling, you also want to change speeds. Practice the step-over move that Portuguese superstar Cristiano Ronaldo (top) has perfected. After you complete the move, go in the other direction with a burst of speed.

Swing your leg around and just above the ball in one direction. This will get the defender to lean in the direction you are faking.

After your fake, push the ball in the opposite direction with the outside edge of your foot.

4 SHIELDING

Sometimes you simply cannot fake out your opponent. You can still maintain control of the ball by shielding it with your body. To do this, keep the ball close to one of your feet and as far away from your opponent as possible. Stand sideways to your opponent. Expect to be bumped by your opponent. Extend your arm slightly toward your opponent without committing a foul. Do not push with your arm or jab with your elbow. Keep your body between your opponent and the ball. Look to pass to a teammate. Or, if you get the chance, break free with a sudden burst of speed.

Brazilian national team player Daniela shields the ball from U.S. national team defender Stephanie Lopez during the 2007 FIFA Women's World Cup. It is important to shield the ball when pressured by defenders with your back to goal.

DID YOU KNOW?

Juggling is keeping the ball in the air with your feet or other "legal" body parts (not your hands!). It takes a lot of practice. A few keys to good juggling: Keep your feet flat. Use your thighs when the ball goes up as high as your chin. Use alternating feet. Dan Magness of England holds the world record for juggling a ball in the air for twenty-four hours straight. How long can you do it?

Juggling is a great way to practice your foot skills and your first touch. You can use your feet, thighs, chest, and even your head to keep the ball in the air.

5 RECEIVING

Before you can keep control of the ball, you must gain control of it. Receiving the ball requires touch. When a pass skids to you, if you hold your foot steady, the ball will likely bounce off it and roll away. You want to "catch" the ball by pulling your foot back in the direction the ball is headed. This is called settling. Your foot becomes like a cushion. The ball touches your foot softly and settles near it.

Before you can dribble or pass the ball to a teammate, you must be able to receive or trap the ball. Your foot should be like a cushion, allowing the ball to settle near you.

An advanced trick is trapping the ball by lifting your foot and pinning the pass to the ground with the bottom of your foot. You can also receive the ball with your thigh, chest, or head. You can control it softly with any of these other body parts by pulling them back in the same manner as with your foot.

If you know what direction you want to go with the ball, you can start in that direction even before receiving the pass. This is called first touch. In this case, you can keep your foot firm and let the ball carom off it in the direction you want to go. Or you can run at the ball while receiving it with your chest and continue running as it moves forward with you.

THEN AND NOW

In the early days of soccer, the field was as much as ten miles long, with the game played by entire villages. Today, soccer fields are between 100 and 130 yards long and between 50 and 100 yards wide.

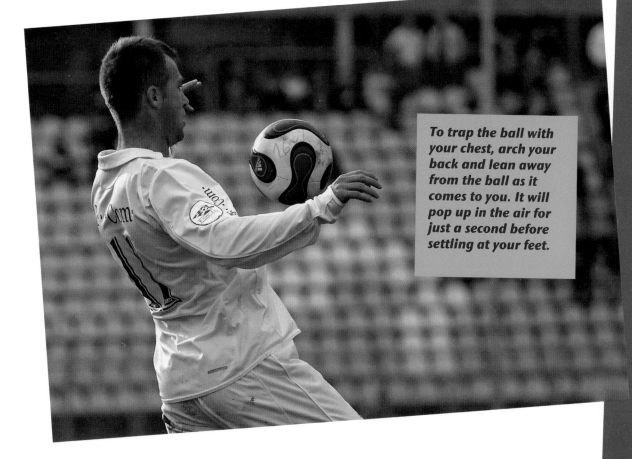

To trap the ball with your chest, arch your back and lean away from the ball as it comes to you. It will pop up in the air for just a second before settling at your feet.

PASSING

Soccer is a team sport. Sharing the ball with your teammates gives you the best chance to win. Passing is a smart way to move the ball toward the goal. To make a good pass, you must spot your target, then watch the ball as you kick it. Accuracy is the key. If your teammate is moving, kick it where he or she is going to be. If you do not have the ball, get open.

6 THE BASIC PASS

All basic passes start with the non-kicking foot. You "plant" this foot into the ground by stepping firmly behind and to the side of the ball. Your plant foot should be pointed in the direction of your kick. Your body weight should shift onto your plant foot. Your kicking foot is now able to swing freely.

The easiest pass to make is the push pass. It is a short-distance pass of about ten yards or less. You should turn your kicking foot sideways and strike the ball with the inside of your foot. You should try to kick squarely into the middle of the ball or slightly above middle to move it swiftly along the ground. Be sure to follow through with your kicking leg in the direction of the pass.

Strike the middle of the ball with the inside of your foot.

Point your plant foot in the direction you want to pass the ball.

Technique is more important than power when making a short pass. Once you feel comfortable passing with your strong foot, spend extra time practicing with your weaker foot.

7 THE POWER PASS

Longer passes require more power. You want to approach the ball as you would a push pass. But after planting your foot, your technique changes. Bring your kicking leg as far back as you can while keeping your balance. As you begin your kick, your leg should be headed more over the ball, with your knee bent. This allows you to whip your lower leg into the ball with force. Many beginning players try to kick hard with their toes. This is a mistake. You cannot kick accurately with this part of your foot. You want to strike the ball with the instep of your foot. The instep is the inside middle of your foot beneath your shoelaces.

You can send a power pass along the ground or through the air. To keep the kick low, place your plant foot alongside the ball. Strike the ball slightly above the middle. Keep your knee moving forward over the ball. To lift the ball into the air, plant your foot to the side but several inches back from the ball. Stop your knee short of moving over the ball. Strike the underside of the ball. As you make contact, lean your body back slightly.

PRO TIPS AND TRICKS

Landon Donovan is arguably the greatest soccer player ever for the United States. He has starred in three World Cups. Donovan knows the value of passing. "I used to focus more on scoring," he says. "Now I take a lot of pride and pleasure in helping someone else do well too." Donovan's two sports heroes growing up were hockey's Wayne Gretzky and basketball's Magic Johnson. Why? "The thing I liked most about them," Donovan says, "is the fact that they passed the ball [or puck] extremely well."

Instep

When you want to make a longer pass, use your instep like Landon Donovan is doing in this photo. Keep your arms out for balance and follow through the ball. Donovan's great passing ability helped lead the United States to the knockout stage in the 2010 FIFA World Cup.

8 FANCY PASSING

Sometimes your teammate may be running free, but your opponent is directly in your way. You can use a trick pass to get the ball past your opponent.

A chip pass is a great way to bloop the ball over the head of a nearby opponent. Plant your non-kicking foot behind the ball. Extend your arms to provide balance. Keep your knee forward as you kick downward. Your foot should stab at the ball and then jab into the ground. Striking the bottom of the ball at the correct angle should lift it in the air with backspin.

A trickier way to lift the ball over a defender is with the rainbow pass. Place the heel of your right foot on the front of the

ball. Put your left foot under the back of the ball. Roll the ball with your toes up the back of your right leg. Jump in the air off your right foot. Whip your right leg up behind you while keeping the ball on it. Follow through. The ball should flip up and over you and your opponent!

When opponents are blocking your passing lane to a teammate, try to chip the ball over your opponent's head. Make sure to lean back and strike down at the bottom of the ball to lift it in the air.

The rainbow pass (shown here) is a more advanced trick. It's a great skill to practice on your own.

9 PASSING STRATEGY

Sometimes it is wise to pass in a direction other than directly toward your goal. The best way forward often starts backward. When your path is blocked and you cannot lift the ball over your opponent, you simply make a basic pass backward to a teammate. Turn your body sideways and kick the ball with your instep. Or turn in the opposite direction and whack it with the outside edge of your foot. To save time, you can pass backward without turning your body simply by rapping the ball with your heel. This is more difficult, so you must practice it.

In any case, immediately after you pass, you should run to an open area and look for a return pass. This is called a give-and-go. It is also known as a wall pass, as though your teammate is a wall, and you are kicking the ball off "the wall," so that it can bounce back to you.

THEN AND NOW

In the early 1960s, National Football League place-kickers approached the football straight on and kicked with the toes of their foot. In 1964, Pete Gogolak joined the Buffalo Bills of the AFL. He kicked the ball "soccer style" by approaching it at an angle and kicking with his instep. Gogolak's kicks were so accurate that he helped the Bills win the league title. Today, all pro football kickers are "soccer style" kickers.

10 THROW-INS

When a player on one team knocks the ball out of play beyond the touchline (sideline), a player on the other team must throw it back onto the field. The throw-in can be a weapon if it is done properly. Be sure to hold the ball equally with both hands. Start with your hands behind your head. Your teammates should be scrambling to get open. Get a running start. Launch both arms and your upper body forward with force as you throw the ball. Keep both feet on the ground as you release. If you lift either foot, it is an illegal throw. Don't stand and admire your throw—jump into the action!

DID YOU KNOW?

Unless you are a parrot, you are likely right-footed. Ninety percent of parrots are left-footed. Ninety percent of people are right-footed. It is hard to tell watching pro soccer players whether they are right-footed or left-footed. They practice using their opposite foot enough so that they can control the ball equally with either foot.

Glen Johnson, a defender on England's national team, displays the proper form for a throw-in. Follow the proper form because if you commit an illegal throw-in, the other team gets the ball.

SHOOTING

Fine dribbling and smart passing will move the ball toward the goal. But how do you put it in the back of the net? There are many ways to shoot. The key is to do it quickly. See your chance and—bang—let it fly!

11 WHERE TO SHOOT

Many beginners shoot the ball at the middle of the goal. This is a mistake. This is where the goalkeeper is! It is nice to have a powerful shot, but the goalkeeper can stop even the hardest shot if it comes right at him. Placement is more important than power. You want to kick the ball to spots where the goalkeeper is not.

You want to aim your shots low and wide or high and wide. These are the four corners. Choose the corner that appears most open and shoot at it. Be sure to aim a foot or so inside the post and below the crossbar. Remember, the hardest shot ever that goes too high or too wide is still a missed shot.

THEN AND NOW

Edison Arantes do Nascimento is widely considered to be the greatest goal scorer in history. He played in the 1960s and 1970s for Brazil. He is better known by his nickname—Pelé. Among today's greatest goal scorers are Argentina's Lionel Messi, Spain's David Villa, England's Wayne Rooney, and Portugal's Cristiano Ronaldo.

Just before you shoot, pick your head up to see where the goalie is standing. Maybe the goalie is leaning in one direction or is out of position. Pick a target and fire away!

An opportunity is lost when a shot is taken too early, too late, or not at all. If you have a clear shot, and you can reach the goal with some force—shoot! Do it right away. Do not stare at your target. Do not shift your stance so you can kick it with your "better" foot. Do not back up to kick it. Do not pass it to a teammate because he or she has a stronger leg. Just remember the four-corners rule, see the goalkeeper and the goal, and fire away!

There are also times when you should *not* shoot. If you are far from the goal, you might improve your team's chances of scoring by looking for a teammate running toward the goal. Make a quick pass. Break for the goal. Your teammate may be able to give it back to you. Another time to hold your shot is if you are within range, but the goalkeeper is right in front of you. Here is your chance to try a trick move, such as the inside turn, outside turn, or step-over. Hurry, before defensive help arrives.

DID YOU KNOW?

A goal is scored only when the entire ball crosses over the goal line. Even if most of the ball is across the line, but the back end of it is on the line, it is not a goal.

During a game, the opportunity to score will pass by in a split second. You must be ready to shoot right away. Defenders will not give you time to line it up or think about where to aim. U.S. national team striker Jozy Altidore fires a shot before Spain defender Carles Puyol can block it during the Confederations Cup in June 2009.

13 SHOOTING LOW AND HIGH

Shooting at the lower corners and upper corners requires different techniques. To shoot low, plant your foot to the side and slightly ahead of the ball. Your upper body should be upright or even slightly leaning forward. Swing your leg down and through, keeping your knee bent and moving forward over the ball. Keep your foot pointed down. At the moment just before contact, whip your lower leg through the ball. Strike the ball with your instep. Connect with the middle part of the ball or slightly above middle. Follow through with your kicking leg staying close to the ground.

To shoot high, plant your foot to the side and behind the ball. Keep your body upright until impact, then tilt it back. Your leg should straighten with your knee locked. Connect with the lower part of the ball. Follow through and high. When kicking hard, try to land on your kicking foot. This will add power to your shot.

Shooting accurately and powerfully requires a lot of practice. Samuel Eto'o (pictured here), a striker from Cameroon, practiced hard to become one of the best goal scorers in the world.

Have your arms out for balance and lean forward to keep a shot low; lean back slightly to have your shot go higher.

Make sure your toes are pointed down and your ankle is locked.

Keep your plant foot next to the ball, aimed at your target.

Your shooting technique will change slightly depending on whether you are aiming high or low. However, never lean back too far or you'll see all your shots soaring over the goal.

14 TRICK SHOTS

There are moments when it seems you do not have time or an opening for a shot. Or do you? What if you could shoot without ever controlling the ball? What if you could curve a shot around a defender? The answer is, you can.

When the ball comes at you, and you don't have time to settle it, you can just shoot it in the air before it ever touches the ground. This is called a volley shot. For this shot, timing is everything. Extend your arms to keep your balance. Point your foot down and keep your knee above the approaching ball. Meet the ball in the air with the inside of your ankle. Your kick should be a quick, compact movement. The speed of the ball coming at you will provide the power. A half-volley shot is similar. If the ball bounces just before it gets to you, simply kick it with the same technique as the volley shot. Try to strike the ball when it is rising.

If a defender or the goalkeeper is in your way, you may be able to shoot around him by bending the ball. Approach the ball as you would to shoot high. Lean backward and away from the ball. Point your toes slightly up. Kick the outside of the ball with the inside of your foot. The ball should spin and start bending in. Or, kick the inside of the ball with the outside of your foot. The ball should spin and bend out. Remember to kick the ball on the side that is opposite the direction you want it to curve.

PRO TIPS AND TRICKS

Time was running out for England. They needed a goal to reach the 2002 World Cup. Superstar David Beckham had a free kick from 25 yards out. The Greece defenders formed a wall in front of him. Beckham approached the ball wide from the left and kicked the right side of the ball with the inside of his right foot. The ball flew high and to the right of the goal. Suddenly, it swerved to the left. Its flight curved so much that the goalkeeper could not get to it. The ball went inside the left post for a goal. Beckham's ability to bend shots even inspired a movie that year called *Bend it Like Beckham*. Beckham tells young players to practice bending shots because they are nearly impossible to stop.

David Beckham strikes a free kick during an exhibition game as a member of the Los Angeles Galaxy of Major League Soccer (MLS). Beckham is a master at bending the ball. This is a trick shot you can practice, and perhaps someday you will master it, too!

The ball is often in the air. There are times when you simply don't have time or space to let it drop. In such cases, performing a header is the perfect trick.

Heading the ball is safe, as long as you use proper form. As the ball approaches, position your body directly in front of it. Clench your teeth so you don't bite your tongue. Keep your eyes on the ball. Pull your head and upper body back, then thrust forward to meet the ball. Strike the ball with the upper front part of your forehead. This is the area near the hairline. Keep your eyes on the ball as it makes contact with your head. Watch its flight.

A great time for a header is off a corner kick. Your teammate should send a lofted pass in front of the goal. If you run forward and time it right, you can score with your forehead. That's using your head!

In the heat of a game, you will need to fight for position to win a header. When jockeying for position with your opponent, watch the flight of the ball. Time your leap so you head the ball at the highest point of your jump. Keep your arms up to protect yourself, but do not swing them around or push off because you can be called for a foul.

Your eyes should be open; head the ball with your forehead.

Arch your back and neck as the ball is coming and thrust yourself forward when it arrives.

Heading the ball is an important part of soccer on both offense and defense. You may need to use your head to score the game-winning goal or to stop the other team from scoring.

DEFENDING

So much attention in youth soccer is placed on scoring a goal. Preventing a goal deserves equal credit. If you stop your opponent from scoring, you cannot lose the game. Defenders are just as important as goal scorers. Playing solid defense requires teamwork and focus.

16 GETTING IN POSITION

As a defender, you want to be between the ball and the goal. This is the most important individual strategy for a defender. Always remind yourself of this.

If an attacker has the ball, you want to thwart the attack quickly. Sprint to a spot a few steps in front of the attacker, putting your body between the ball and the goal. Slow down by shortening your stride to close in carefully those last few steps. This is called containing. If you sprint all the way up to the attacker, it is easier for the attacker to make a sudden change of direction and go past you. You want to move in with urgency, yet under control. Keeping yourself in front of the attacker allows defensive help to arrive.

If your attacker is especially skilled, you can work with a defensive teammate to form a double team. In this case, your approach should be from an angle, with your teammate at the opposite side. This is called funneling. Together you can close in on the attacker. The touchline also serves as an extra defender. If your attacker is near the touchline, approach him or her at an angle that forces your opponent toward the touchline.

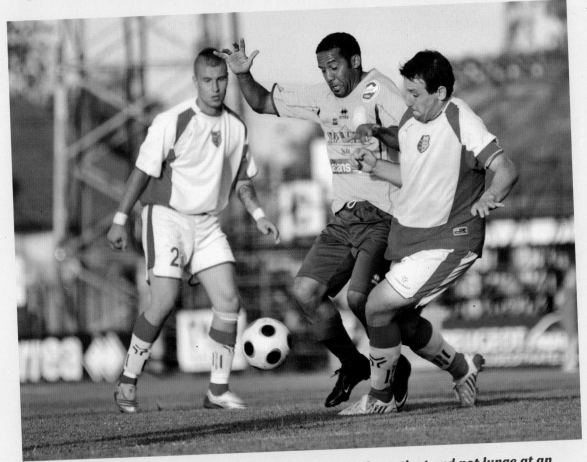

Good defense in soccer requires many things. You must be patient and not lunge at an attacker's fakes. However, you must also be aggressive when the time is right. Always stay between your opponent and the goal. Try to force your opponent to his or her weaker foot. When you think you can tackle the ball, go for it!

17 DEFENDING IN CLOSE

Once you have moved in front of the attacker, it is time to put your best defensive skills to work. Most youth players spend so much time practicing tricky dribbling moves. This is the opposite of that. You can foil those tricks with your smart play. Position your body in a crouch. Stay low with your feet wide, knees bent, arms extended, facing the attacker. Be ready to react. Do not act on the attacker's fakes. Focus on two spots—the attacker's midsection and the ball. As that midsection shifts, shift with it. Be like a mirror. As for the ball, if the attacker shields it with his body, move in and make contact with the attacker. Lean on him with your shoulders, but don't use your elbows. You can frustrate your opponent this way. Just be sure to play within the rules.

THEN AND NOW

Early professional soccer featured attacking offenses and more scoring. Of the eleven players on a side, usually only two were used for defense. Today, in addition to the goalie, four other defenders are often on the field.

18 TACKLING

Tackling in American football is taking down the player with the ball. Tackling in soccer is taking away the ball itself. You do not want to overcommit and lose containment. But you do want to take the ball away. Timing is everything. If you think you can get to the ball and tackle it—go for it! Just don't tackle the player, too, because that is illegal.

The safest type of tackle is the toe poke. You can do this when your attacker is shielding you. Use the toe of your foot that is closer to the ball to poke it away. A block tackle is similar, except you use the inside of your foot.

A slide tackle is more difficult. Some youth leagues do not allow it. If it is legal, you should learn to use it. Approach the ball with a running start from directly in front of your opponent or from the side. Go into a feet-first slide, as you would in baseball. Your lower leg should be bent at the knee and skidding along the ground. Your upper leg should be extended. Kick the ball away with your extended leg. Be careful not to kick your opponent. Never attempt a tackle from behind.

A slide tackle is often your last chance as a defender. If you think your opponent has you beat and can take a shot or make a pass, that might be the best moment to try a slide tackle. Never go into a slide tackle with your cleats up and do not tackle from behind.

19 WHERE TO KICK IT

Once you have regained control of the ball, where should you kick it? It depends where you are on the field and what is in front of you. If you are in the penalty area, you have only one choice—kick it away from your goal! This is no place to dribble. You cannot afford a mistake here. Kick it high and wide. This is called clearing it.

If you are a bit farther up field, you have options. If opponents are surrounding you, kick it over the touchline. This gives your teammates time to get in position to help you defend. If you have an open teammate nearby, pass it. If you have clear space in front of you, dribble it. Push it forward as far as you can until defenders come to challenge you. Many beginners often simply kick it down the middle to no one in particular. This is a mistake. Either team could gain possession. Always try to keep control of the ball. Except, of course, when you need to clear it!

The best defenders in the world must work hard to stop dangerous attackers like Lionel Messi (right). Defenders must stay low, knees bent, and watch the ball. It also helps to study your opponent. If you're on the bench, watch the players you will be going up against. See what they like to do and force them to do the opposite when you're in the game.

PRO TIPS AND TRICKS

Philipp Lahm of Germany stands just 5 feet 7 inches tall. Still, many consider him the best defender in world. He is proof that you can be great at any size. Lahm is famous for hustling. Even the best defenders get beat. When an attacker beats Lahm, he spins and sprints back to defend the attacker again.

Once you take the ball from your opponent, look up the field for an open teammate. If you cannot find anybody open, clear the ball high and wide.

20 GOALKEEPING

If you are the goalkeeper, you are your team's last line of defense. You get to wear a colorful jersey and touch the ball with your hands or any other body parts (while you are in the penalty area). But you also get extra pressure. You must be focused and aware of a few tips.

To start, you should be a few feet in front of the goal, standing with your feet shoulder-width apart, knees slightly bent, ready for anything. To stop a group of attackers, you should move forward and back or side to side so that you are between the ball and the center of the goal. To stop a single onrushing attacker, you should carefully go out to meet him or her to cut down on the angle.

Use your hands when you can. To stop a rolling ball, move behind the ball and drop to one knee. Keep your hands close to the ground, fingers wide and pointed down, thumbs touching. Scoop the ball and hug it. To stop a rolling ball away from you, dive head-first, extend an arm, and punch it away. To stop a ball in the air to you, get behind it, bend your elbows, fingers wide and pointed up, thumbs touching (this is called the "W"). Catch the ball and hug it. To stop a ball in the air away from you, jump off one leg and punch it away. If a ball is loose amid a flurry of players, and you think you can get to it—go out and get it!

Once in possession, you have six seconds to get rid of it. Run out to the eighteen-yard line with it. Kick or throw it to a teammate. Keep possession, when you can.

DID YOU KNOW?

In professional soccer, a team stops eight out of every nine shots attempted.

To catch the ball, form your hands into a "W" with your thumbs touching.

A goalkeeper must be ready and aware at all times. When the ball is shot on goal or crossed into the penalty box, you must decide if you can catch it or if you should punch it away.

GETTING READY TO PLAY

Playing soccer can be a wonderful experience, especially if you spend time preparing yourself. Here are a few more tips to give you an extra edge.

21 STRETCHING

To protect your legs from injury, you should stretch. Before stretching, it is important to warm up to get your blood flowing. Jog with the ball a bit to practice your touch. Now you are ready to stretch. First, take a wide stance. Reach down and touch the ground in front of you. Now touch the ground directly below you. If you can, reach to touch behind you. Next, stand normally. Lift one foot behind you and grab it with your hand. Pull up to stretch the front of your leg. Finally, stand with your feet shoulder-width apart. Squat down so that your thighs are parallel to the ground, keeping your heels on the ground. Spring into the air as high as you can. Perform ten of these squat jumps.

DID YOU KNOW?

Except for the goalie, a pro soccer player runs about five miles in a game. You probably run at least half that in yours.

It is a good idea to warm up before playing a game or practicing. After you loosen up, stretch out your legs. Even the pros stretch before they play.

22 NUTRITION

It is a good habit to eat well regularly. It is especially important before a soccer match. You don't necessarily want to eat a full meal right before the game. But you should eat something healthy at least an hour before. If your game is in the morning, have a bowl of cereal and a piece of fruit. If it starts in the afternoon, have a sandwich and fruit. Before the game starts, drink plenty of water. Don't wait until you are thirsty. During the game, drink more water. Eat a piece of fruit at halftime. Skip the snacks until after the game.

Preparation is very important in soccer. You want to eat right, pay attention at practice, and always work hard.

23 PRACTICE

Some players treat practice as a time to goof off. Don't let this be you. For instance, your coach may have you and your teammates form a line to practice a dribbling drill. Standing for two minutes waiting for your turn can be boring. Use the time to watch your teammates. Chances are you will learn something. No matter what your coach has you do for practice, always give your full attention and your best effort, just as you would in a game.

To really improve, you want to practice on your own, as well. It can be as simple as repeatedly kicking the ball against a wall. For an extra challenge, try kicking against a tree—it will require accuracy and a quick reaction for unpredictable bounce backs.

THEN AND NOW

Pro soccer's biggest event is the World Cup, which is held every four years. The first World Cup was in 1930 with thirteen nations participating. The host nation of Uruguay won the final. Today, the tournament features the top 32 nations out of more than 200 who try to qualify. The 2010 World Cup was played in South Africa. Spain beat the Netherlands in the final, 1–0.

The Spanish national team celebrates its victory at the 2010 FIFA World Cup final.

24 PREGAME

The game is starting in a few minutes. Maybe your team went for a fun jog in tight formation. Maybe you stood in line and took a few shots at the goal. You certainly want to do what your coach tells you. But you also want to be ready to sprint! Are you warmed up enough? If you don't think so, and you have the chance, set your soccer ball next to you. Jump sideways over it. Jump several times back and forth that way. Now jump front to back. Sprint to a nearby tree or to fetch a few loose balls. Are your teammates excited? You can help. Try this simple act on one player: Smile, clap your hands, and say, "Are you ready?" Your enthusiasm may rub off.

Hard work, a positive attitude, and teamwork will make for a fun soccer experience.

25 ATTITUDE

The game is under way. You want to do your best. How? Give your ultimate effort every minute. Never walk when you should run. More important, remember that soccer is a team sport. You want to help your team win. If you score a goal—good for you! Just remember to thank the teammate who passed the ball to you. If someone else scores, congratulate them with a smile, and compliment the player who made the assist. Win or lose, praise your teammates for their effort. Thank your coach. Be positive. Your attitude will make your soccer experience a success.

PRO TIPS AND TRICKS

England's Wayne Rooney and Argentina's Lionel Messi are two of the best players in the world. Messi says it is Rooney's passion and work ethic that makes him great. "There are always a handful of players in the world at any one time who can go down in the footballing [soccer] history books," Messi says. "At the moment, there are maybe Cristiano Ronaldo, Rooney, Xavi, and one or two more. I can't think of one that plays with the desire of Rooney. You can see the fire in his eyes. It's that fire which makes him the best of the best."

GLOSSARY

★**clearing**—Kicking the ball out of danger to prevent an opponent's scoring chance.

★**containing**—Keeping yourself between your opponent with the ball and your goal.

★**crossbar**—The pole that forms the top of the goal.

★**funneling**—Approaching your opponent with the ball at an angle to force him or her toward your teammate or the touchline.

★**half-volley**—Kicking a ball after it has just bounced.

★**instep**—The inside middle of your foot beneath your shoelaces.

★**plant foot**—The foot that steps onto the ground before the ball is kicked with the opposite foot.

★**post**—The two poles that form the sides of the goal.

★**settling**—Controlling a pass by bringing it softly to the ground.

★**shielding**—Keeping possession of the ball by positioning the body between an opponent and the ball.

★**touchline**—The sideline that marks the boundary on either side of the field.

★**volley**—Kicking a ball out of midair.

★**wall pass**—A pass to a teammate who passes it back to you. Also called a give-and-go.

FURTHER READING

Books

Beckham, David. *David Beckham's Soccer Skills*. New York: Collins, 2006.

Drewett, Jim. *How to Improve at Soccer*. New York: Crabtree Publishing Co., 2008.

Gifford, Clive. *Soccer: The Ultimate Guide to the Beautiful Game*. Boston: Kingfisher, 2004.

Rediger, Pat. *Soccer*. New York: Weigl Publishers, 2010.

Stewart, Mike and Mike Kennedy. *Goal: The Fire and Fury of Soccer's Greatest Moment*. Minneapolis, Minn.: Millbrook Press, 2010.

Thomas, Keltie. *How Soccer Works*. Toronto: Maple Tree Press, 2007.

Internet Addresses

Soccer Training Info
<http://www.soccer-training-info.com/default.asp>

U.S. Soccer
<http://www.ussoccer.com/>

U.S. Youth Soccer: Skillz School Videos
<http://www.usyouthsoccer.org/players/SkillzSchoolVideos. asp>

INDEX